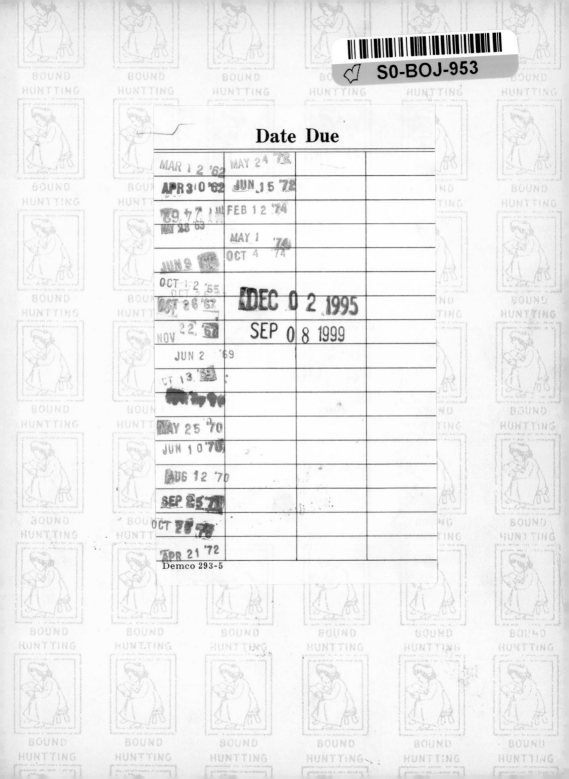

A Trip

To Hawaii

First Edition
Commemorating the admission of
Hawaii
our fiftieth state
into the United States of America

ACKNOWLEDGMENTS

The author wishes to thank the following for cooperation in providing information, photographs, and other assistance in the preparation of this book:

HAWAII VISITORS BUREAU

Hawaiian Sugar Planters' Association

Pineapple Companies of Hawaii

U. S. Navy, Fourteenth Naval District

Aloha Airline

Honolulu Star-Bulletin, Ltd.

The Honolulu Advertiser

The Waikiki Beach Press

Department of Public Education, State of Hawaii

Special thanks to TRIPPIE and JEFF, and others who posed for photographs, as well as the many other kind friends who helped make this book possible.

Special photography by Paul Seaman

A TRIP

TO HAWAII

by Carla Greene 11493

LANTERN PRESS, Inc.
Publishers
257 FOURTH AVENUE   NEW YORK 10, N. Y.

CONTENTS

J
99 6
G

9-14-61

A View of Honolulu Harbor

LAND AHEAD!

"Hurry! Let's get up on deck!" urged Jeff and Trippie Allen's father. "Arriving in Honolulu Harbor is a sight you will never forget."

After traveling a little more than four days on a modern ocean liner, across the sparkling blue Pacific, the great moment had arrived. The Allen family would soon be landing at Honolulu, the capital of the Hawaiian Islands, and one of the most beautiful cities in the world.

There are eight major islands in the Hawaiian group. In order of their size, they are: Hawaii, known as the big island; then Maui, Oahu, Kauai, Molokai, Lanai, Niihau, and Kahoolawe. In addition, there are a number of smaller uninhabited islands.

While the city of Honolulu is on the island of Oahu, only third in size, it is the largest, most modern, and most populated city of the islands.

What a thrill it was for Jeff and Trippie to see the towering mountains on the island of Oahu come into view!

"I read a book that said the Hawaiian Islands are really mountaintops," said Jeff.

"Yes," said his father, "the islands were formed by great volcanic explosions under the sea. The mountains rise as high as fourteen thousand feet above the sea, and perhaps go twice that deep below."

"Imagine!" gasped Trippie. "Hawaiians live right on top of a volcano!" '

ALOHA—with Flowers and Music!

Soon, just ahead, Trippie and Jeff could see the extinct volcano, Diamond Head. The whole harbor came to life with little boats. Brown boys swimming beside the ship were shouting *"Aloha,"* the warm Hawaiian greeting which means either hello or good-by.

Mr. Allen gave Trippie and Jeff some coins. "Toss them overboard," he said.

Swiftly, a half dozen heads bobbed under the water and dived down, appearing again with the coins clutched between their teeth.

Soft strains of music floated up from the shore. The Royal Hawaiian Band, which meets all ships, was playing *"Aloha Oe,"* the famous song which was written by the last queen of Hawaii.

As the ship docked, there was a great rush of island people laden with flower wreaths to greet the visitors. It is a charming Hawaiian custom to hang a wreath of colorful, sweet-smelling flowers on each guest, with a kiss on the cheek and a warm "Aloha." The wreaths, called *leis*, are made of a variety of the most beautiful island flowers—orchids, carnations, plumeria blossoms, or, the sweetest smelling of all, small white *pikake* flowers.

At first, Jeff felt foolish. He protested, "I don't want to wear flowers like a sissy." But soon he noticed boys

and men wearing leis as well as girls and women. Some
had so many they could hardly raise their chins over them.

"When you are in Hawaii," Trippie advised him,
"you had better do as the Hawaiians do."

HAWAII — our Fiftieth State

The first sight that Jeff and Trippie saw as they drove away from the pier in a taxi, was a tall tower with the word ALOHA across the front.

"It feels good to be so welcome in a foreign country," remarked Trippie.

"For Pete's sake!" exclaimed Jeff. "You should know better than to call Hawaii a foreign country. Don't you know that Hawaii is now our Fiftieth State?"

Trippie felt a little ashamed. "Of course, I know it," she said. "I just forgot because I have been seeing so many different kinds of people."

"The Hawaiian population is a mixture of many races," said Mr. Allen. "Most of the people are from the Orient. There are few pure Hawaiians."

Mr. Allen was right. Over forty per cent of the people in Hawaii are Japanese, about seventeen per cent are part Hawaiian, and about fifteen per cent belong to the white race. The white people are called *haoles*. The rest of the population is divided between Chinese, Puerto Ricans, Filipinos, Samoans, and others. In more than half a million people in the islands, pure Hawaiians make up only about two per cent of the population.

"The people of Hawaii are true Americans," Mr. Allen went on. "The children speak English in the schools.

Aloha Tower

Hawaiians call the American continent the *mainland*. They call us visitors *malihinis*. The old-time settlers are called *kamaainas*.

"Even though Hawaii is more than two thousand miles from the mainland," Mr. Allen continued, "the Hawaiians feel very close to us. Speedy jet planes will make the distance seem shorter still."

HONOLULU—a Large, Modern City

As they rode through downtown Honolulu, Jeff and Trippie were surprised to find it such a large, modern, bustling city. Autos, buses, taxis, bicycles, and people on foot filled the streets.

"Gee, I expected to see grass shacks," said Trippie.

Mr. Allen laughed. "Grass shacks belong to primitive Hawaii," he said. "Honolulu is now a city of about three hundred thousand people. It is very much like a city on the mainland."

"They're not wearing grass skirts either," remarked Jeff.

"No," said his sister, "but I notice many of the women are wearing strange-looking long full dresses."

"Those are *muu muus*," said Mrs. Allen. "I read in a magazine that they are dresses styled after the Mother Hubbard dresses of missionary times. Most Hawaiian women wear them around their homes, but the visitors to the islands like to wear them everywhere, because they are so cool and comfortable."

"Let's get some," said Trippie. "I think it would be fun to wear one of these splashy printed dresses."

Downtown, the Allens saw big banks, department stores, restaurants, drugstores, a five-and-ten-cent store, the telephone and electric company buildings, and many other important modern structures.

Downtown Honolulu

13

"What's that?" exclaimed Trippie suddenly. She pointed to a huge golden pineapple on a rooftop.

"It's a big tank on top of the world's largest cannery, where island pineapple is canned," said her father.

"Is it filled with pineapple juice?" asked Jeff eagerly.

Mr. Allen laughed. "No, it's just a water tank. But we'll visit the pineapple cannery some day, and you can drink all the fresh pineapple juice you want, right out of a faucet."

"That's for me!" said Jeff. "I can't wait!"

WAIKIKI—and the Beautiful Beach!

As the taxi headed out toward Waikiki, where the Allens were going to stay, smaller places of business appeared all along the route. There were fruit and vegetable stands, grocery stores, flower shops, and many others. Some stores had signs in Japanese or Chinese, because many of the island's inhabitants come from those countries.

In about ten minutes the Allens reached their hotel at Waikiki, one of the most famous resort areas in the world. As many as one hundred and sixty thousand visitors make the trip to the Hawaiian Islands in a single year, and each year there are more and more. Many new hotels are being built at Waikiki, to accommodate them.

A visitor's time is usually divided between seeing the many interesting sights and enjoying the beach and water sports which the Hawaiians have loved from the earliest primitive times. And, of course, everyone goes shopping in the beautiful stores that line the avenue just back of the beach area. Eating in the many different kinds of restaurants—Hawaiian, Chinese, Japanese, Korean, or American—is a large part of the fun of a visit to the islands.

"What a gorgeous view!" cried Trippie, when the Allens checked into their rooms at the hotel overlooking

the Pacific. The climate is warm and balmy most of the year in Honolulu, so the sliding glass door, which formed the end wall of the room, was completely drawn aside. The ocean looked like a sparkling blue sapphire, crested with whitecaps. And there was Diamond Head, just a spear's throw away.

"Let's go swimming!" cried Jeff.

"Oh yes, let's go swimming right away!" Trippie exclaimed.

Mr. Allen, who had been stationed in the islands during World War II, warned: "The sun's rays are very hot at this time of the day. It's easy to get sunburned and spoil our vacation. Why don't we go sight-seeing for a while and then swim when we get back?"

Mrs. Allen agreed that it would be a better idea to go sight-seeing first, but Trippie and Jeff didn't like to put off the swimming.

"We can learn a great deal about the early life of Hawaii at the Bishop Museum," encouraged Mr. Allen. "You will see a real grass shack there."

"A grass shack!" cried Jeff. "O.K., I guess I can wait to go swimming."

Trippie wanted to see a grass shack too, so she agreed, and the Allens took a bus ride to the Bishop Museum. They arrived there just in time to join a group who were being guided through the museum by a cheerful, plump Hawaiian woman, named Kilani.

LIFE IN EARLY HAWAII

How exciting it was to see the real grass shack! Kilani, the guide, explained that this early Hawaiian house was made of a framework of trunks of slim trees. A thick thatch of *pili* grass was tied to the framework to cover the sides and roof. The roof was built to a peak to shed rain. The walls were closely woven to shut out the wind.

"You will notice that there is no chimney," said Kilani. "In this mild climate, there was no need to have heat in the houses, and the cooking was done outdoors. The people used their houses only for sleeping or to protect themselves from rainy weather. They slept on the ground, on the mats which they wove of *lauhala*, leaves of the *hala* tree."

Kilani pointed out an old wooden bowl with a stone pounder, which was used for pounding *poi*.

"The early Hawaiians practically lived on fish and poi," said Kilani. "The poi was made from *taro*, a root plant that looks something like a sweet potato. The taro was steamed or baked, then pounded with water until it became a light purplish mass, like bread dough, called poi. The poi was wrapped in leaves and put away in wooden pots. When it was time for a meal, a chunk was taken out, and water was added to make a thinner paste.

Early native pounding poi

The paste was put in a bowl, and each person dipped into the bowl with his fingers and licked off the poi."

Kilani went on: "Hawaiians today still eat poi, instead of bread, with practically every meal, but now most poi is ground in a factory and sold in stores. The Hawaiians make one-finger, two-finger, or three-finger poi, indicating the thickness of the paste, and how many fingers it takes to pick it up."

Trippie spied a carved wooden paddle with a handle.

"What is this?" she asked.

"It's a beater which the ancient Hawaiians used to make their cloth, called *tapa*," said Kilani. "They stripped the inner bark from the young mulberry trees and soaked it in water for several days. Then they put three or four strips of bark over each other and pounded them with the wooden beater until they formed a pulp. By constant beating, the pulp flattened out into the tapa cloth that looks like paper."

Kilani pointed to a piece of tapa hanging on the wall. It did indeed look like paper.

"The colored designs were beaten into the cloth with dyes which were put into the grooves of the beater. To make the tapa rainproof, it was dipped into oil made from *kukui* nuts," she said.

The friendly guide went on to tell that the tapa cloth was used for the clothing of the early natives. "The man wore a long strip of cloth called a *malo*. He wrapped it around his waist and between his legs. The woman wore a cloth skirt reaching from the waist to the knees. It was called a *pa'u*."

"Where did the Hawaiian people come from originally?" asked Trippie.

Kilani was pleased to hear the question. She always liked to tell the story of the daring natives, led by *Hawaii Loa*, who settled the Hawaiian Islands. This is the story she told:

Early native beating tapa

"Although the islands have been in existence for many thousands of years, it is believed that the first native settlers were Polynesians from the South Seas. They arrived about fifteen hundred years ago, in about the year A.D. 400.

"The Polynesians were a daring, seafaring people who sailed thousands of miles from the South Pacific in light canoes which they made themselves from hollowed out logs of the *koa* tree. The canoes had outriggers made of poles from the flexible *wili wili* tree. The outriggers kept the boats from tipping over easily. But these men needed more to keep afloat in the great, stormy Pacific. These early, bold seamen knew many things about nature.

"They watched the positions of the stars, the sun, and the moon. They understood the movement of the ocean currents. They followed the flights of birds. They knew just how to knife through the waves in their canoes, which were designed for this purpose. With all this knowledge, which they passed on by word of mouth from generation to generation, they were able to sail thousands of miles with safety."

"What did they do for food on these long journeys?" asked Jeff.

"The Polynesians had always been an island people who lived around water, so they were excellent fishermen. They lived on the fish they caught and the fruits and other food plants which they took along."

Kilani went on: "The Polynesians kept arriving in the Hawaiian Islands for a couple of hundred years; then they seem to have stopped. The only record of these early settlers is in the legends which were handed down about them.

"These early settlers were said to be tiny people, not more than two or three feet tall, called *Menehunes*. Although they were small, they were very strong and built canals, stone walls, temples, and fishponds of lava rock. They are supposed to have worked only after dark and had to finish in one night any job they began. Anything that was not completed by sunrise was left unfinished forever. Some of the works of the Menehunes are still seen in the Islands today.

"Several hundred years passed," Kilani continued, "before more settlers arrived in the Hawaiian Islands. Then, in about the year 1000, Polynesians began to arrive by the thousands. These newcomers brought the first pigs, chickens, and dogs to Hawaii. They brought plants which are grown in the islands today—coconut, banana, breadfruit, taro, and others. Unlike the early settlers, who were tiny, these more recent Polynesians were tall, strong, brown-skinned people. They are said to have been more civilized than the early natives, and they became the ruling class or *ali'i*."

"How did the early Hawaiians do their cooking?" asked Mrs. Allen, who was interested in cooking even when she was on a vacation.

"The natives dug a hole in the ground and lined the bottom and sides with rocks, making an oven called an *imu*. They kindled a fire by rubbing sticks together. When the rocks were heated, they roasted fish, birds, or chickens in the oven. For special feasts, they roasted pigs and dogs, both of which were treats to the early Hawaiians. The feast was called a *luau*."

"I hear Hawaiians still give luaus," said Mrs. Allen.

"Yes, indeed," Kilani assured her. "Hawaiian families give luaus for the birth of a child, a wedding, Christmas, or just for fun, almost any time. Some of the hotels and restaurants give luaus for our visitors. You must go to one while you are here."

In a large case in the museum, the Allens saw a statue of a Hawaiian native making a fishing net from the fibers of the *olona* plant.

"Fishing was always a necessity for living in the islands, and the net was either spread by men in canoes or it was thrown by hand," Kilani said. "Throw-net fishing is still a popular sport. It takes strength and skill. The fisherman stalks his prey, then throws the weighted net over the water. The fish are caught in the net, and the fisherman wades in and brings the catch to shore.

"The early natives built fresh-water fishponds. They put the live fish they caught into these ponds and bred them for future use. Some of these fishponds, which are more than a thousand years old, are still to be seen around the islands today.

"Another early form of fishing," Kilani continued, "is torch fishing at night. If you look out over the water almost any night, you will see the torches of the fisher-

men, who still enjoy night fishing.

"The primitive fisherman used a torch lit with oil from the kukui nut. Today, most of them use modern acetylene torches. The fisher probes among the coral rocks for a bright-colored food fish, which is attracted by the light from the torch. He spears the fish just as his ancestors did.

"There is an old-time superstition that goes with night fishing," Kilani went on. "When a man goes torch fishing, his wife is not supposed to tell anyone that he has gone. She is not to quarrel with anyone or gossip. If she disobeys these rules, the fish will hide, and her husband will not be able to catch any."

"Here is one of our most precious possessions," said Kilani pointing to a handsome cape made of feathers in gold and black. "Feather capes were worn by royalty and chiefs of the ruling class. Each cape, as you can see, was made of thousands of tiny feathers. It took many months, or even years, to make one of these capes. First, a net was woven of fibers from the *olona* plant. Then each feather was tied on separately."

"How did they get the feathers?" asked Trippie.

"There were men who were feather hunters," said Kilani. "They knew the trees where certain small native birds would perch. The hunters covered sticks with vegetable glue and put them into the trees. The feet of the birds got stuck to the sticks. The hunters would then climb the trees and pluck small tufts of feathers from the birds' tails. Then they let the birds go free, so they could grow more of the same feathers for the next season."

Kilani then showed them a chief's helmet made of feathers and some tall sticks adorned with feather tops. The sticks were called *kahilis*.

"Here is how a chief looked," said Kilani. "This is a picture of a modern Hawaiian dressed for one of our Aloha Week parades, which are held every year in October. You will notice that the kahilis are carried by the chief's attendants."

Early Hawaiian feather cloaks at the Bishop Museum

Feather cloak worn in Aloha Day parade

HAWAIIAN WATER SPORTS

When the Allens returned to the hotel, Jeff said eagerly, "Hurry, let's get into our bathing suits. I want to swim in the ocean."

How refreshing it was to get into the clear salt water. The water was placid and shallow, and the Allens could walk out a long way. But ahead of them they could see tremendous waves breaking.

"Why are the breakers so far from the shore?" Jeff asked.

"There are great reefs of coral out there," said his father. "When the waves hit the reefs, the waters rebound and make the tall breakers."

"Look," shouted Trippie. "Here come some surf-board riders." The surfers skimmed over the waves on their surfboards like swift racers. They came riding into shore at about thirty miles an hour.

"How do they get their surfboards way out there?" Jeff asked.

"Look over to your left," said his father. "See those boys lying flat on their stomachs on their boards? Watch them paddle with their arms until they get out beyond the breakers. Then they will stand up on their boards and ride in on the waves."

"It looks easy," said Jeff. "I would like to try it."

"It's not easy," said Mr. Allen. "The young Hawaiians make it look easy, because they do it so skillfully. Most of them begin to learn when they are small children. They get year-round practice in this fine climate."

"I sure would like to try it," said Jeff.

"We'll get one of the surf-riding teachers to give you lessons," promised his father.

"Look, look!" Trippie shouted. "Here comes an outrigger canoe. How I would like to swoop over the waves like that!"

"Wouldn't I?" chimed in Jeff. "Dad, couldn't we go for a ride in an outrigger?"

"I understand we can rent one on this beach," said Mrs. Allen. "Let's all go."

Mr. Allen found that there would be an outrigger for rent in about a half hour, and that two Hawaiian young men, called beach boys, would go out with them. Jeff and Trippie could hardly wait!

What a thrill it was to ride in the outrigger! The beach boys, named *Kala* and *Luka*, showed the Allens how to paddle, on opposite sides, just as the ancient Hawaiians had paddled the same type of canoe for thousands of miles.

After paddling out beyond the breakers, they turned the canoe around, and it came shooting swiftly back to shore over the crest of the waves.

"Whee!" shouted Jeff. "This is like riding a roller coaster!"

"We were riding thirty miles an hour," said Kala, when the canoe slowed down near the shore.

"Let's do it again," said Trippie with enthusiasm. They went back and forth several times. Each ride was more thrilling than the last one.

After their exciting ride, the Allens stretched out on

the beautiful white sand beach.

The sun was beginning to go down, and a gentle trade wind was blowing. The palm trees swayed gracefully in the breeze. Gradually, the sky began to turn into beautiful shades of pink and purple, and the Allens saw one of the glorious sunsets for which the islands are famous.

"Oh," sighed Trippie. "I would like to paint this."

Jeff decided to have fun burying Trippie in the sand.

Suddenly Jeff spied a strange-looking boat. It looked like two canoes with a platform and a sail.

"Hey! What's that?" he exclaimed.

"It's a catamaran," explained his father. "Many of the later settlers of the Hawaiian Islands arrived in these double canoes, instead of the single outriggers. They sailed more safely and were able to bring many of their plants and animals along."

"What is it used for now?" asked Trippie.

"It's a pleasure boat," said her father. "They have moonlight sails."

"Oh, let's go tonight!" urged Trippie.

"No, let's save this for another evening," said Mrs. Allen. "We have had enough water sports for one day."

A modern Catamaran

EVENING AT WAIKIKI

When the Allens got back to their hotel rooms, the sunset had changed into twilight. Soon it was evening. Trippie and Jeff changed their clothes, and went out on the terrace while they waited for their mother and father to get dressed.

All along the beach below, they could see tall torches flaming softly. Every evening, Waikiki Beach is lit for miles with old Hawaiian torches burning oil, which gives a romantic flickering light.

"Where is the music coming from?" asked Trippie. They looked down and saw a group of Hawaiian young men and ladies strumming *ukuleles* and singing softly.

The ukulele, which is a favorite in Hawaii, was brought there by the Portuguese. Ukulele means "leaping flea," and it was named that because the fingers leap across the strings so quickly and lightly. This instrument and the Hawaiian guitar are heard everywhere in the islands today.

When Mr. and Mrs. Allen were ready, the family went to dinner at a restaurant on Kalakaua Avenue, the main street of Waikiki. The Allens tried out some of the many kinds of food served in Hawaii.

Trippie ordered *mahi mahi*, the delicious dolphin which everyone tastes at least once in the islands. Jeff had *teriyaki* steak, a Japanese dish of meat cooked with ginger and other tasty spices.

Mrs. Allen had half of a huge pineapple scooped out and heaped with many kinds of delicious fruits. Mr. Allen said: "I'm going to be brave." He ordered squid, a small octopus which is considered a delicacy in Hawaii.

After dinner, the Allens took a walk along Kalakaua Avenue and stopped to look at the wares on the native stands which stood along the sidewalks. Hawaiian women were selling lovely jewelry they had made themselves from many kinds of seeds and shells. Some women were sitting with baskets of blossoms and stringing leis, which they hung in rows on their station-wagon stands. A man sat carving funny heads out of coconuts.

"I see some of the shops are open," said Mrs. Allen. "This would be a good time to buy some of the bright Hawaiian clothes all the mainlanders seems to be wearing."

Mrs. Allen bought a long loose muu muu for Trippie. For herself, she bought a fitted dress called a *holomu*. Mr. Allen and Jeff bought some bright printed shirts called aloha shirts, which most of the men visitors were wearing.

HISTORY AT THE CIVIC CENTER

The next day, the Allens put on their Hawaiian clothes and went sight-seeing at the Civic Center near downtown Honolulu.

Grouped around the Civic Center, the Allens found all the important government buildings and the beautiful public library. In front of the courthouse stood a mammoth statue of a warrior in a golden cloak and helmet, glinting in the sunshine. The name on the statue read KAMEHAMEHA I.

Kamehameha I was the great warrior who conquered and united the Hawaiian Islands. He is also known as Kamehameha the Great, and is loved and respected by Hawaiians as the mainlanders revere George Washington.

Until Kamehameha I set out to unite the islands, there were many different kings. Each king was the ruler of an island, or part of an island. Each king owned all the land he ruled over. Under the king was a class of nobles, called the *ali'i*, consisting of chiefs, chiefesses, and priests. Under them, were the common people.

Kamehameha I was about twenty years old when the first white man arrived in Hawaii.

CAPTAIN COOK
DISCOVERS THE ISLANDS

In 1778 Captain James Cook, the English explorer, sailing about the South Seas, sighted the islands with their high mountain peaks, and knew that he had made a great discovery. He landed his two sloops, the *Resolution* and the *Discovery*, on the island farthest north, Kauai. Captain Cook named the islands the Sandwich Islands, after the Earl of Sandwich, in England, who had sponsored many of his voyages.

The Hawaiian natives, who had never seen white men before, believed them to be gods. They fell on their knees before the white men.

It was easy for Captain Cook to make friends with the natives. One of the things which the Hawaiians needed most were tools and utensils made of iron. They had only stone or bone pots and pans and weapons. Captain Cook gave them the things they needed, and they gave him food supplies, fish, fruits, and vegetables.

Captain Cook and his men stayed only two weeks on this first visit. A year later, however, they returned and set up quarters on the west coast of the big island of Hawaii. Again, they were treated like royalty.

But soon a problem arose. Because the early Hawaiians prized things made of iron so highly, some went so far as to steal small iron tools from the ship. Then, one night, a group of natives made off with a small boat from the ship *Discovery*. While they had plenty of small boats of their own, this one was made with iron nails, and they wanted to break it apart for the nails.

Captain Cook became angry. To punish the men who had stolen the boat, he invited their king aboard his ship, then held him for the return of the boat. The warriors of the island rose to the defense of their king, and a battle took place between them and Captain Cook and his crew. Captain Cook was killed in the battle.

It was shortly after the *Resolution* and the *Discovery* sailed back to England without their captain that the young chief, Kamehameha, began his rise to power.

In about 1780, his uncle, the aged king of the island of Hawaii, gave up his throne to his son, Kiwalao. Kamehameha, who was a cousin, was given a position second in power. After a short time, Kamehameha and several other chiefs became discontented and led a rebellion against Kiwalao. He was killed in battle, and Kamehameha became king.

Kamehameha had learned much from the visit of Captain Cook, and he wanted to unite the islands under his rule. For ten years, his warriors fought the kings and chiefs of the various islands, until at last Kamehameha became accepted as king of all the islands.

After he began his rule of the islands, Kamehameha I

made it his business to see that the houses were rebuilt, the crops replanted, and that people were put back to work at their crafts. He even tilled the soil himself, as an example to his people. He became greatly honored and beloved as a leader of his people.

In 1792 George Vancouver, an English explorer, who had been on one of Captain Cook's ships, made a return visit to the islands. He brought grapevines, orange trees, and other fruit and vegetable seeds and plants, which are grown to this day. He also brought the first cattle to the islands.

King Kamehameha welcomed Vancouver, and they became very good friends. Wisely, the king gave orders that none of the cattle should be killed for ten years, thus starting a long-term supply of meat and milk products for the islands.

Soon the Hawaiian Islands became a stopover point for many ships from Europe and America. In 1803 the first horses were landed from a trading vessel. In about 1810, sandalwood trees, which grew in the islands, were bought by ship captains and sold in China, where the wood was burned on the altars for its fragrance.

The sandalwood trade grew rapidly and brought great wealth to Kamehameha I. But when he found that the supply was becoming almost completely exhausted, he passed a law that no young trees were to be cut down.

Kamehameha I ruled wisely and did much to help

his people. He passed laws against attacking anyone, and against stealing, murder, and other crimes. When he died in 1819, a new era began in Hawaii.

About one year after Kamehameha I's death, the New England missionaries arrived in Hawaii. Seven couples with five children, together with four Hawaiians who had been attending school in America, set sail in a small ship from New England. They had to make a long, dangerous journey all the way around Cape Horn to reach Hawaii. The trip took almost six months. Their safe arrival was a very important step in the progress of Hawaii.

Upon the death of Kamehameha I, his son Liholiho became king, and was known as Kamehameha II. But the power behind him was his father's widow, the Queen Mother. She was a wise woman with advanced ideas. Even before the missionaries arrived, she had influenced the people to give up many of their old superstitions and idol worship. She welcomed the missionaries and encouraged them in teaching the Christian faith.

THE MISSIONARIES
BRING RELIGION AND EDUCATION

The missionaries began at once to preach the Christian faith and educate the natives. As soon as the missionaries learned the Hawaiian language, they set about putting it into English letters, and the Hawaiians for the first time began to read and write their own language.

The Queen Mother was one of the first to learn to read and write. She set an example to her people, for soon everyone — old and young alike — wanted to learn. At first the missionaries set up schools in grass shacks. Not only did they teach reading and writing, they taught the natives how to grow farm products. They taught them the building trades also, and soon the natives were helping the missionaries to build schools and churches.

At first they made wooden buildings, but after a while, they constructed churches of huge rocks.

At the Civic Center, not far from the heroic statue of Kamehameha I, the Allens saw three old wooden houses. In front of the biggest house they saw a sign saying that it was the oldest frame house in Hawaii, built in 1822 by the New England missionaries. Next to the big house was a smaller building with an old printing press in it. This was the press used by the missionaries to put

Mission houses

Kawaiaho Church

the Hawaiian language into English letters and to spread
the Christian religion in Hawaii.

Next to the mission houses, the Allens found the
most famous of the old churches, Kawaiahao Church,
built in 1841 and still in use today. State funerals for
Hawaiian kings and nobility were held there, and most
of their burial places are there. It is often called the
Westminster Abbey of Hawaii.

Across the way from Kamehameha's statue, at the Civic Center, the Allens visited Iolani Palace, the only royal palace on American soil.

More than sixty years packed with events had passed between the time when the missionaries landed and the building of the palace, in 1881.

After just a five-year reign, King Kamehameha II died. His younger brother became Kamehameha III. He reigned from 1825 to 1854, and in the twenty-nine years of his rule much progress was made in Hawaii.

Up to this time, the king had always owned all the land. But many new settlers brought new ideas from the outside world. The Hawaiian people began to expect better opportunities. Kamehameha III divided his land into three parts. He kept one third and gave one third to his chiefs and one third to the people. He even went further and gave half of his own share to the people, and some of his chiefs did the same.

During this period, however, many problems arose in Hawaii. In about 1826 the great whaling fleets began to make Hawaii a stopover point. The sailors and merchants who came ashore, after long periods at sea, became drunk and disorderly. The missionaries were very much opposed to this, and they persuaded the Hawaiian chiefs to set up a code of laws, a constitution, a legislature, and courts of law.

Before the arrival of the white man, there had been

Iolani Palace

no germ diseases in the islands. Now the natives were dying by the thousands in great epidemics of diseases brought by the foreigners. When Captain Cook had first arrived in the islands, there were almost half a million people. At the time of Kamehameha III's death in 1854, there were only seventy-five thousand native inhabitants left in the islands.

KAUAI

LIHUE ●

OAHU

HONOLULU

DIAMOND HEAD

NIIHAU

HAWAIIAN ISLANDS

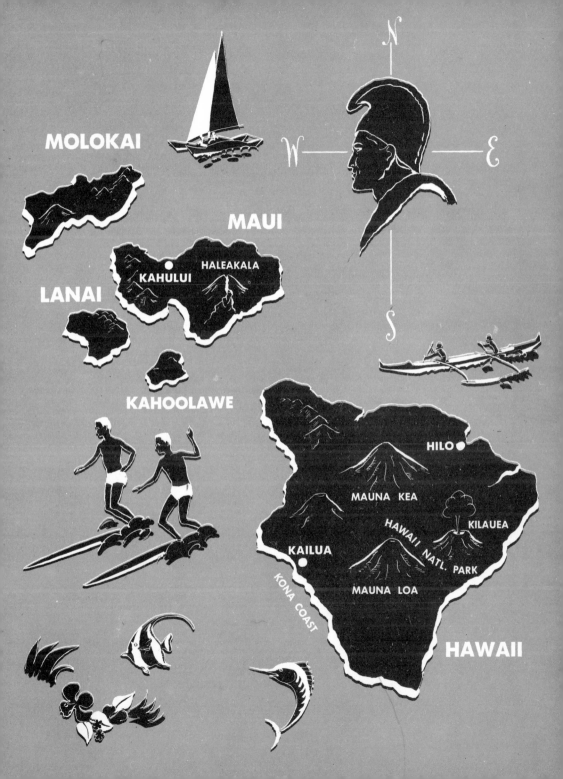

The king's adopted son became Kamehameha IV. To preserve the Hawaiian people, the new king and his wife, Queen Emma, set about educating the people in the rules of health. They built the Queen's Hospital in Honolulu to care for the sick. To this day, patients of Hawaiian blood are cared for there.

In spite of all precautions, Kamehameha IV died after only an eight-year reign, at the age of twenty-nine.

In 1863 his brother became Kamehameha V. His nine-year reign was not popular, because he wanted a powerful monarchy instead of the liberal government which had been established. After a long struggle, he managed to regain some of the royal authority.

When Kamehameha V died in 1872, there was no direct heir to the throne, because he had been a bachelor. It was necessary to hold an election. Prince Lunalilo, who promised to reinstate the liberal constitution, was elected. Unfortunately, he died after only one year.

Again an election was held. A Hawaiian noble, David Kalakaua, was elected, and began his reign in 1874. At first, he seemed to be a good king. He signed a much-needed treaty with the United States, allowing Hawaiian sugar to be shipped into the United States without duty. This was the beginning of the growth of the most important industry in Hawaii.

King Kalakaua, who was called the "Merry Monarch," loved pomp and splendor. He built Iolani Palace at a cost of $350,000. He also indulged in other extravagant spending, leaving the treasury short of money. He brought his government into great disfavor. After much battling, a reform party forced him to put a new constitution into force that took away all his political power. Then Kalakaua's health failed. He went to San Francisco for medical treatment, and died there in 1891.

The Allens found Iolani Palace still in use by the Hawaiian government. The governor's office is in Kalakaua's bedroom. The Senate meets in the state dining room. The House of Representative meets in the beautiful throne room.

Soon, however, there will be a new building ready for the government offices, and Iolani Palace will become a museum.

Throne room in Iolani Palace

FALL OF THE MONARCHY

Queen Liliuokalani

Along the corridors of Iolani Palace, the Allens saw oil portraits of kings and queens of the islands. Outstanding was the portrait of Queen Liliuokalani, the last ruler of Hawaii.

The Queen, who was the sister of Kalakaua, began her rule upon his death in 1891. The country was in a state of great unrest. Some felt that it was time to end the rule of kings and to start a republic. Others wanted to make the powers of the rulers strong again, as they were during the early days of the kingdom.

Liliuokalani was a woman of great charm and talent. She was a composer and musician, and wrote many of the most beloved Hawaiian songs, including the famous *Aloha Oe*. But she sided with those who wanted to strengthen the monarchy, and many Hawaiians, as well as the large number of foreigners, who by then were leaders in the business of the islands, opposed her.

For more than a hundred years, different nations had been trying to take over and govern the islands. England, France, and Russia had made attempts. But the United States was located closer to the islands and had many Americans active in politics and business there, so she had the best opportunity.

On January 17, 1893, the Hawaiian Annexation Party took over the government by force. Queen Liliuokalani was taken prisoner and held in an upper room in Iolani Palace. She was imprisoned for nine months, but instead of bemoaning her fate, she spent her time composing songs which are still sung in the islands today.

On July 4, 1894, the Republic of Hawaii was set up with Sanford B. Dole as president. The republic lasted for six years, during which time the plan to annex Hawaii to the United States went on. After many delays, the annexation took place, and the republic was given up.

In 1900, President McKinley appointed Sanford B. Dole the first governor of the islands. After that, for more than half a century, the President of the United

States appointed the governor, the secretary, and the judges of the important courts. The people of Hawaii elected a representative to the Congress of the United States to look after their interests, but he had no vote. Neither did the people of Hawaii have a vote for the President or Vice-president of the United States.

When Hawaii became a territory of the United States in 1900, the population was about a hundred and ten thousand people. In a little over fifty years, the population increased five times, to more than half a million.

For many years, Hawaiian leaders fought for the right of Hawaii to become a state. They pointed to the many brave residents of the islands who had seen active duty in the United States Armed Forces. They reminded Congress that the people of Hawaii paid the same taxes as other American citizens. Why then should they not have the same voting rights?

At last, the dream of the Hawaiian people came true. On March 12, 1959, the bill providing for Hawaiian statehood was passed by Congress. Shrill sirens, bells, bonfires, and joyous dancing in the streets greeted the wonderful news! A fiftieth star was added to the United States flag. Now Hawaii has the same rights and privileges as any other state in the union.

HULAS AND MUSIC

The next morning, Mrs. Allen said, "They are having a *hula* festival at one of the parks. Shall we go?"

"Yes," cried Trippie. "I'm dying to see some real hula dancers!"

The hula festival was very colorful. An announcer described the dances and their meanings.

The Allens learned that there are many different kinds of hulas, and different kinds of music to accompany them. Most of the dancers were young women, but there were men dancers too.

Some of the dancers performed hulas that go back to ancient Hawaii. These were religious dances, and the dancers beat out rhythms on gourds, which they carried. As they danced, they spoke long chants, called *meles*, telling stories about their ancient gods and goddesses. These dancers wore the costumes of the primitive Hawaiians.

Some of the dancers performed more modern hulas to popular tunes such as "Little Grass Shack," or "Lovely Hula Hands," which were played for them on ukuleles or guitars. The girl dancers wore skirts made of *ti* leaves and told stories with graceful motions of the hands, while swaying their hips like rippling waves.

The announcer explained that certain motions meant clouds, rain, love, food, or other words. In this way, a whole story was told through the dance.

There were hulas from Tahiti or Samoa, which were very fast and exciting. The dancers wore skirts of dried grass that looked like straw.

Some of the hulas were danced in long dresses, such as were worn when the missionaries came and insisted that the dancers cover their bodies.

Children learn to hula at very early ages in Hawaii. They love to perform for special occasions, and they especially like to do comic hulas. Some girls and boys danced a comic hula. It was great fun to watch them.

When the hula dancers had completed their performance, the announcer called out: "All visitors please form a line and we will teach you the hula."

Almost everyone joined in. It was a riot of fun, especially watching some fat men trying the dance!

Afterward some of the dancers showed off other native skills.

A young man scampered up a coconut tree and down again, as fast as a squirrel. He showed Trippie and Jeff how to open a coconut to drink the milk.

Coconut tree climber

Some of the natives sat in a circle and wove coconut hats. Others made mats of lauhala. Some made flower leis.

Coconut hat makers

Making flower leis

INTERNATIONAL MARKET PLACE

Right in the heart of the Waikiki shopping area, the Allens found a quaint place with ancient idols at the entrance and many kinds of buildings—grass shacks, pagodas, a quaint little bridge, and various trees and flowers. It was the International Market Place.

"This is like taking a trip around the world," said Mrs. Allen, as they discovered shops and restaurants representing a wide variety of Pacific countries. Here was a native wood carver making artistic heads of koa wood; across the way, was a Japanese tea garden; nearby, a Chinese gift shop.

"Look at this strange tree," said Trippie.

"It's a banyan tree," said her father. "Notice how the branches drop to the ground. Then they take root and grow into new tree trunks. It's said the banyan trees were first brought here from India. There are several very famous ones on the island of Oahu."

"Look, there's a little house up in the tree!" exclaimed Jeff. Sure enough, there was a stairway leading up to a little tree house. Mr. Allen asked one of the shopkeepers about it, and he was told that people could reserve the house and have dinner served from one of the famous restaurants. The price? Well, Mr. Allen decided it was too high for their budget.

The Allens under the banyan tree

IDOLS AND LEGENDS

At the entrance of the International Market Place, and in various spots around the grounds, the Allens found carved idols. Mr. Allen took a picture of Trippie and Jeff near one of them.

"These are some of the gods that were worshiped in ancient Hawaii," said Mr. Allen. "The early settlers had many gods and half-gods in their Polynesian backgrounds. They told about them in long, poetic chants that were handed down by word of mouth from generation to generation."

"I would like to know what some of those legends were," said Trippie.

"There are a number of good books relating the old legends," answered her father. "One of the most well known legends is about Madam Pele, the goddess of fire."

"Can you tell it?" challenged Jeff.

"I'll try to tell it briefly," said his father. "Pele is said to have lived in the crater of Diamond Head when it was an active volcano. When the volcano erupted, the natives believed that Pele was angry. Later, Pele is supposed to have moved to other volcanoes. Her most recent home is supposed to be on the island of Hawaii. We'll see some of Pele's work when we visit the other islands next week."

"I read that when chunks of crystal were found at the foot of Diamond Head, they were said to be Pele's tears," remarked Mrs. Allen.

"Yes," said Mr. Allen. "But some sailors thought they had discovered diamonds. When the king heard about this, he passed a law that no one except royalty would be allowed to step on the premises. When it was found that the sparkling pieces were not really diamonds, the ban was lifted, but the mountain was named Diamond Head just the same."

AQUARIUM AND ZOO

One day, the Allens passed the aquarium.

"They must have lots of tropical fish in there," surmised Jeff. "Let's stop and see them."

Jeff was right. Never had he and Trippie seen such a collection of beautiful tropical fish. There were striped fish, sea stars, sea urchins, sea cucumbers, and many forms of reef life. The fish that amused them most of all was a very tiny one with the longest name in the world. It was called the *humu-humu-nuku-nuku-apu-aa.*

"If you can learn to say that word, you'll be an expert in speaking Hawaiian," said Jeff to Trippie.

Not far from the aquarium, the Allens found the zoo. They saw a mongoose, a small brown animal that was brought to the islands to get rid of rats. Now the mongoose is so plentiful that some islanders say they would like to get rid of these animals too.

The Allens also saw some wild mountain goats, wild pigs, native owls, tremendous turtles weighing hundreds of pounds, and other animals and birds that are found in the islands.

PIG IN THE IMU

"There is a real Polynesian luau at one of the big hotels," said Mr. Allen. "If we go there about noon, we can watch them put the pig in the imu—that's the underground oven."

The Allens reached the hotel grounds just in time to see the festive procession of young men carrying the pig to the imu, the pit in which it would be cooked for many hours. The young men all wore bright printed skirts, called *lava lavas*, and colorful leis of flowers. Two trumpeters blew weird notes on conch shells. Two of the men carried the pig hanging upside down on a decorated pole. The pig wore a big bow tie.

"Jiminy, I have to get a picture of this!" said Jeff.

The colorful group stopped and posed for Jeff. Many other people took pictures too. Then the procession went ahead to the blasts of the conch shells and rat-a-tat of the drum.

The Allens followed, and found several more young Hawaiians busy arranging red-hot lava rocks on top of the log fire. Some of the hot rocks were put inside the pig's body. Net wiring was put into the pit, and banana leaves were spread over it. Then the pig was lowered into the pit. Sweet potatoes and bananas were added. The pig was covered with wet ti leaves, moist burlap, and earth.

"Now," said Mr. Allen, "the pig will steam under the earth for hours."

"When do we eat it?" asked Jeff anxiously.

"We will come back to the luau at about six o'clock this evening," said his father. "It would be a good idea to spend the afternoon swimming so we can work up a good appetite."

THE LUAU — a Wonderful Feast

At six o'clock, the Allens went to the feast. Beautifully decorated tables were placed low so that everyone sat on tiny flat stools close to the ground. Everyone had part of the delicious steamed pig, many kinds of fish, yams, coconut pudding, pineapple, bananas, papaya and, of course, poi, the old Hawaiian stand-by that goes with every meal.

"I wish I had a bigger *opu*," said Jeff, patting his stomach.

PARADISE OF FLOWERS AND TREES!

The next day, Mr. Allen said, "If you want to see how beautiful Oahu Island really is, we should take some trips. I'll rent a car, and we can drive to different places."

Mrs. Allen looked over a folder that told of interesting sights.

"Here's something," she said. "Robert Louis Stevenson's grass hut."

"Did Stevenson live on Oahu?" queried Jeff in surprise.

"It seems he did," said Mrs. Allen. "And it says that Mark Twain spent some time here too. Here is what he called Hawaii: 'The most beautiful fleet of islands that lie anchored in any ocean.'"

"Hmm," said Trippie, "no wonder my teacher told me we were going to visit the Paradise of the Pacific."

As the Allens drove along in the rented car, it was easy to see why so many people, including those not so famous as Mark Twain, loved the islands for their beauty.

The houses, most of them as modern as any on the mainland, were set in a riot of tropical flowers and graceful trees of almost endless variety. Each house seemed to be made for outdoor living, with a porch called a *lanai*, where the family could eat or just enjoy the mild, fragrant air.

"Oh my goodness," Mrs. Allen gasped. "Look at the exquisite orchids! There are so many. No wonder the Hawaiians can afford to make whole leis of them."

"What are those?" cried Trippie, pointing to some glossy heart-shaped blooms.

"They are anthuriums, also called elephant ears," said Mr. Allen. "They are very rare and expensive on the mainland."

Riding along, the Allens saw giant poinsettias, flowering ginger, bird-of-paradise flowers, roses in every color, gardenias, carnations, and the mysterious white cereus which blooms only at night.

Growing in thick hedges around the houses in almost

Girls with hibiscus in hair, tending a taro patch

Orchids grow in many colors

every color imaginable was the official flower of Hawaii, the hibiscus. There are hundreds of varieties of hibiscus in Hawaii today. The women love to wear them in their hair—over the left ear if they are single and seeking romance, over the right ear if they are married.

The Allens saw many unusual trees too: shower trees loaded with their colorful blooms; wide-spreading, gnarled monkeypod trees, from which the Hawaiians make smoothly polished wooden bowls and trays; hala trees, from which they make woven mats, baskets, bags, and floor coverings; strong, tall palm trees loaded with coconuts; breadfruit, papaya, avocado, and banana trees; guava, orange, lemon and lime trees; and trees heavy with macadamia nuts, a new product in the islands.

Anthuriums or elephant ears

Night-blooming cereus

Wide-spreading monkeypod tree

It's fun to pick breadfruit

Papayas grow on a tall tree

Plumeria tree in blossom

Amusing sausage tree

"Here is the University of Hawaii," said Mr. Allen. "Students from all over the world come to study here. The campus is very beautiful. Let's stop and look at it."

"What a funny tree!" exclaimed Jeff, as they walked through the campus grounds. "It has sausages hanging from it." He was right. The tree had long gourds that look like sausages and is called the sausage tree.

The Allens saw many other varieties of plants and trees, for there are literally thousands of different kinds growing in Hawaii.

Every now and then, as they drove along, they saw a post topped with a Hawaiian warrior head. These are markers one finds throughout the islands, pointing out places of interest to visitors.

"Have you noticed that we haven't seen a single advertising billboard yet?" asked Mrs. Allen.

"And you won't," her husband assured her. "Billboards are outlawed in Hawaii, because they spoil the view."

At last, the Allens came to the grass hut which had been the home of Robert Louis Stevenson.

"Stevenson is my favorite author," said Jeff. "Seeing this hut makes me want to learn much more about his life, especially in Hawaii."

PUNCHBOWL—a National Cemetery

Next, the Allens drove to Punchbowl, the large, bowl-shaped crater of an extinct volcano, which is now the National Memorial Cemetery of the Pacific. Thousands of our dead of World War II and the Korean conflict are laid to rest there.

There is a beautiful view of the city from Punchbowl. Mr. Allen pointed out the important points.

The family walked around in the cemetery and Mrs. Allen looked for the name of her brother who was killed on Wake Island. She found it on a tablet in a long list of names.

A MODERN HAWAIIAN FAMILY

"I would love to see how a real Hawaiian family lives," remarked Trippie the next day.

"I have some old friends here," said her father "If I phone them I am sure they will invite us to call."

The Lahaina family had just sat down to lunch in their back yard when the Allens arrived.

"Please join us for lunch," said Mrs. Lahaina, with true Hawaiian hospitality.

"Thank you," said Mrs. Allen, "we have had our lunch, but we would love to know about your food."

Mrs. Lahaina explained that their main course was called *lau laus*. Each lau lau was made of fish and pork wrapped in ti leaves and steamed. With the lau laus, they were eating poi. The parents were eating with their fingers in the Hawaiian manner, but the boy Akoni, and his sister, Loika, liked to be modern, so they were using little wooden spoons.

Jeff decided that this would be a good chance to find out more about Hawaiian boys and girls.

"Do you play baseball?" Jeff asked Akoni.

"Sure," said Akoni. "I belong to the barefoot baseball team at our school."

"*Barefoot* baseball?" Trippie exclaimed in surprise.

"Yes," said Mrs. Lahaina. "Our *keikis* love to go barefoot most of the time. Most schools allow the children to come to class barefoot until the sixth grade. Their feet get strong and tough. Even some of our best football players kick barefoot."

"Imagine, barefoot football!" said Jeff. "This I would like to see."

"What other sports do you like?" Jeff inquired.

"I like to swim and ride a surfboard," said Akoni.

"I like to climb a coconut tree and drink milk from coconuts. I like to slide down a hill on a slippery ti leaf."

"That's one I never heard of," said Jeff. "How do you do it?"

"We grease the leaves and sit on them, and then go shooting down the hill," said Akoni. "Try it some time."

Akoni's father added, "Sliding down hills goes back to the days of kings. Members of royalty had small sleds, but now the children use leaves."

Trippie asked Loika, "What do you like to do?"

"I like to take part in our school plays and pageants," said Loika. "We celebrate many holidays in school. Besides all the Hawaiian holidays like Kamehameha Day, Lei Day, or Aloha Week, we celebrate the mainland holidays like Thanksgiving and Christmas. Would you like to see some pictures in my album?"

"Oh yes, I would!" Trippie assured her.

It seemed strange to see pictures of children in far-off Hawaii celebrating the old New England Thanksgiving. But it is the mixture of many races and customs combined with the ones we know best that makes Hawaii the fascinating place that it is.

"I like to swim and fish too," said Loika. "And I like to go to picnics. We're going to a *hukilau* next Saturday. I just can't wait!"

"What's a hukilau?" questioned Trippie.

"It's a big fishing party. Everybody helps to pull in the net with the fish. There is a luau afterwards, with lots of good things to eat."

"We would love to have you come to the hukilau with us," Mrs. Lahaina joined in. "Won't you all please come along?"

"Jiminy!" cried Jeff. "Let's go!"

"Thank you," said Mrs. Allen. "I'm sure we would all enjoy going to the hukilau with you."

Before long, Mr. Allen said, "I think we had better be getting along. We have lots of sight-seeing to do this afternoon."

"Aloha. We'll look forward to seeing you on Saturday," said Mrs. Lahaina.

"Aloha, aloha," called Akoni and Loika, waving as the Allens drove off in the car.

SUGAR – Hawaii's Leading Industry

Driving along, the Allens soon came to stretches of miles and miles of sugar cane, waving in the mild Hawaiian breezes. Jeff and Trippie stretched to look up at the high stalks, which grow to about three or four times the height of a full-grown man.

"Sugar is Hawaii's oldest and most important industry," said Mr. Allen. "Sugar was already being grown on several islands when Captain Cook arrived in 1778. The natives liked to chew on it for the sweet taste, just as modern boys and girls of the islands do. It was not until fifty or sixty years later that the first sugar, as we know it today, was produced."

Hand-cultivating sugar

Mr. Allen was right. The sugar industry got its start in 1835 on the island of Kauai, the northernmost island of the Hawaiian chain. There, three New England men leased some land from King Kamehameha III and planted sugar cane. In those days, the planting and cultivating were all done by hand in a slow, laborious way.

It took two years from the time the sugar cane was planted until it was ready to be milled. Iron rollers were brought in from the United States, and the first sugar mill was started. The first shipment consisted of only about two tons of raw sugar, which was sent to the United States to be refined into the pure white sugar we know.

From the very beginning, the sugar industry grew rapidly, and it began to need more and more workers. Because there had been many thousands of deaths owing to the white man's diseases, the Hawaiian population had become very small. The sugar planters had to bring men from other countries to work in the sugar-cane fields and the mills. They brought in large numbers of Japanese, Portuguese, Filipinos, and Chinese.

Some of these workers stayed only long enough to save money and return to their homelands. Many, however, remained, and their descendants today form the largest part of the population of the islands.

Although, it still takes almost two years for a sugar crop to reach maturity, modern machinery and new methods have so improved the planting, harvesting, and milling that sugar has become the largest industry in Hawaii. There are about thirty immense plantations on the islands of Kauai, Hawaii, Maui, and Oahu. They produce more than a million tons of raw sugar each year. The largest part of this sugar is shipped to the mainland to be refined and sold all through the states.

The sugar cane is planted in long furrows which are prepared by modern tractors. Machines cut the cane stalks into one to three-foot lengths. These stalks are planted under about three inches of soil. After two years, the cane is cut, and it need not be replanted for at least four to eight years, as a new crop grows again from the same

root. From two to four crops grow from each planting.

As they got closer, Jeff noticed troughs of water running through the fields. He asked his father about them.

"They are irrigation troughs," said his father. "It takes tremendous amounts of water to irrigate the land to grow sugar cane. They say it takes at least a ton of water for each pound of sugar."

"This cane looks so tall it must be ready to be cut," said Mrs. Allen.

"Yes, it is time for the harvest," said her husband. "Before the cane is cut, men set fire to the field with torches. The fire burns away the leaves but does not harm the stalks which contain the sap. After the burning, the cane is cut by machine, and then big cranes with claws, called grabs, pick up the stalks and put them on trucks to be taken to the mill."

"I would like to see them ·burn the fields," said Jeff. "What a fire that must make!"

"Yes," said his father, "the whole sky is lit up with a red glow. It is quite a sight."

The Allens got back into their car and drove on. Before long, they came to a sugar mill.

"Let's stop and see how sugar is made from the cane," suggested Mr. Allen.

Upon visiting the mill, Trippie and Jeff found that the cane arrives at the mill just a few hours after it is loaded on the trucks.

Harvesting sugar cane

The cane is put onto a moving belt. First, a cane
cleaner sifts out the rocks and dirt. The cane then passes
through a machine with knives that turn and chop the
stalks, and then through rollers that press out the juice.

The juice is mixed with water to help it flow through
pipes from one set of tanks to another.

Each tank performs a separate duty—washing, boiling, purifying, and finally evaporating the liquid—so at
last there is a mixture of sugar crystals and molasses.

Finally, the molasses is separated from the sugar
and is used for animal feed, fertilizer, or in making
alcohol.

The dry stalks which remain are crushed into a pulp called bagasse. This is used as fuel in the factory, or it is made into a product called Canec, a Hawaiian wall-board.

Trippie and Jeff were surprised to learn that it takes one hundred pounds of cane to make twelve pounds of raw sugar. This is put into bins for shipping to refineries on the mainland.

The twelve pounds of raw sugar go through more processes in the refinery, making even less—just a little over eleven pounds of the white sugar we like to use.

Sugar mill

PINEAPPLES — the Second Largest Industry

Driving on, the Allens came to huge fields of pine-apples, growing low on the ground.

The growing and canning of pineapple is the second largest industry in the islands. Almost every family depends in one way or another on the two leading industries —sugar and pineapple.

No one knows exactly when the first pineapples were planted in Hawaii. However, history shows that a Span-iard, Don Francisco de Paula y Marin, planted pineapples in 1813, during the reign of King Kamehameha I.

These early pineapples are said to have been small, tart, and woody. And it was not until some seventy-five years later, that Captain John Kidwell, an English planter, imported a different variety of pineapple, known as the "Smooth Cayenne," probably from the Indies. This is the pineapple grown in the islands today.

The Allens stopped their car and watched a man planting pineapples by hand. They noticed that strips of tar paper were laid in neat rows over the red earth. At regular distances, the man punched a hole into the paper with a sharp iron, then put the top of a pineapple into the hole, and smoothed the earth over it.

"What is the tar paper for?" asked Jeff.

The planter told him, "The paper keeps the soil moist

and warm. It also keeps insects away from the plants and discourages weeds from growing."

Trippie asked, "How long does it take to grow pineapples?"

"The first crop takes about two years," said the planter. "There is a second crop from the same plant, a year later. And there may even be a third crop."

The planter then told the Allens that there was a field of pineapple ready for picking, just a few miles down the road. "Pineapple has to be picked when it is ripe—not a day sooner or later," he said.

As the Allens arrived at the nearby field, Mr. Allen said, "We're in luck. See the men walking along beside the big harvester. They're picking the pineapples."

Trippie and Jeff watched to see how the picking was done. They found that a crew of about ten men were walking along between the rows. As each man picked a ripe pineapple, he broke off the crown and put the fruit on a moving belt which extended from the big boom harvester. The pineapple rode up the boom and was gently dropped into a bin on a truck.

"This is just one of the many new machines in use today in growing pineapple," said Mr. Allen. "There are machines for plowing and harrowing the soil before planting, machines for laying the tar paper, and machines for spraying, fertilizing, and irrigating.

"Some of the most amazing machines are the ones

used in the canneries," Mr. Allen went on. "Just wait until you see the wonderful things they can do."

"We must see the cannery," said Mrs. Allen. "I would certainly like to see how the fine canned pineapple we buy is prepared."

Harvesting pineapple

THE PINEAPPLE CANNERY

The next morning, the Allens visited the world's largest fruit cannery.

A smiling hostess handed them some paper cups and said, "Help yourself to all the pineapple juice you want from this faucet."

"Golly, this is worth a visit to Hawaii," said Jeff.

The Allens found it hard to believe their eyes as they made a trip through the cannery with the hostess. First, they saw the pineapples sorted by machines, according to size. Next, the fruit rode on a moving belt under a shower bath to another amazing machine. In a twinkling, this machine, called the Ginaca, after its inventor, removed the shell, cut off both ends, and punched out the core of the fruit, leaving a golden tube of pineapple.

Next, the tubes of pineapple rode along on moving belts to tables where neat white-capped, white-gloved workers inspected and trimmed each one.

Then another machine sliced the fruit into even rings that looked like doughnuts.

"Just a moment," said the hostess. "We would like you to taste some of this fresh pineapple."

Everyone got a neatly wrapped slice.

"This is the juiciest, sweetest pineapple I have ever tasted," said Trippie.

Pineapple Ginaca machine

"That's for sure," said Jeff, smacking his lips.

The Allens moved on to another group of workers. They were packing the slices of pineapple into cans. They were wearing rubber gloves to keep the fruit perfectly clean.

From there, the filled cans moved on to other machines which added sirup, sealed on covers, and heated and sterilized the contents. Then the cans were cooled, labeled, and packed into cases—all by machine.

"The pineapple that was picked this morning is now ready to be shipped to your stores on the mainland," said the hostess. "Hawaii produces seven hundred and twenty million cans of pineapple products a year. There are slices, chunks, crushed pineapple, pineapple juice, and frozen juice concentrate. The shells are made into cattle feed, and the juice squeezed from the shells is used to produce citric acid."

"It's hard to imagine seven hundred and twenty million cans," said Jeff.

"If they were laid end to end," said the hostess, "these cans would outline the United States—borders, coast line, and all—five times."

"Put your imagination to work on that," said Trippie. "That will keep you busy for a while."

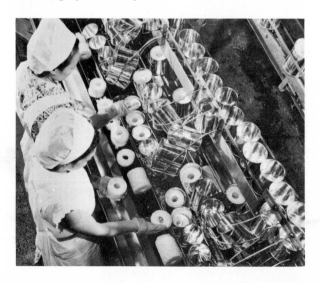

NUUANU PALI — a Historic Cliff

The next day, Mr. Allen said, "We can see one of the most beautiful views in the world from the top of a high cliff called the Nuuanu Pali. Let's drive up there."

"There's history here," said Mr. Allen, as the family got out of the car at a landing near the top of the Nuuanu Pali. "See that marker up near the top of the cliff? That's where Kamehameha I fought the battle that conquered the island of Oahu. The king of Oahu's men were pushed off the cliff to their death."

Nunana Pali lookout

"It takes my breath away just to look down that steep drop," Trippie gasped. "Imagine being pushed down!"

The Pali is two thousand feet high, and the wind blows furiously up there. But the view of the island and its surroundings is amazingly beautiful. Looking through a giant telescope, one can see many tiny islands in amusing shapes, a turtle, a rabbit, an alligator. The Allens took turns looking through the telescope.

Gazing out to sea, Trippie said, "I see a boat out there. It's a flat boat with lots of men on it."

Then her father looked through the lens.

"That looks like a tuna boat," he explained. "Commercial tuna fishing is one of the large industries of the islands. Most of the fishermen are Japanese, and the boat they use is called a sampan. There are some sampans at the yacht harbor near Honolulu. On the way back, we may stop and look at them."

"Let me see," said Jeff, taking over the telescope. "I see lots of birds flying around," he said.

"The birds you see are terns," said his father. "They follow the tuna, and the fishing boats follow the birds. The fishermen throw live bait fishes called 'chum' overboard, so the tuna will follow the boat. Then the fishermen throw out their lines with no bait on the hooks. The tuna are so eager to eat the bait fishes that they bite on the bare hooks and are caught."

Suddenly, it began to rain.

"Oh dear," Mrs. Allen protested, "now our whole day will be spoiled."

"Oh no," her husband assured her. "The rain will be over soon. On the island of Oahu, rain comes and goes quickly. The natives call it 'liquid sunshine' or 'pineapple juice'. Now, if we were on the island of Kauai it might be different. In one part of the island, they get as much as four hundred and sixty-five inches of rain a year."

"Look, look!" Trippie burst forth. "A gorgeous rainbow!"

"I see *two* rainbows," said Jeff excitedly.

"You're making that up," Trippie accused.

But as Trippie looked again, she also saw two rainbows. The double rainbow is seen quite often in the islands. Sometimes there are rainbows even when it hasn't been raining. And sometimes people see rainbows in the evening; these are called lunar rainbows.

The rain stopped as suddenly as it had come, Mr. Allen took the family to see some other famous sights. One was the Upside Down Falls. Here the water rushing down the side of a cliff is caught by strong winds and swept upward, making a waterfall in reverse. It is a remarkable sight!

Another famous sight on the island of Oahu is called the Blow Hole. It is a lava ledge jutting out into the water. There is a natural hole in the ledge, and the action of the waves forces the water up, forming a geyser. Some days the action is greater than others. The Allens were lucky. They saw the Blow Hole in full force. Jeff took a picture of it.

Blow Hole in action

OFF TO THE HUKILAU!

The Allens spent part of almost every day in water sports and on the beach. There were often groups of Hawaiians on the beach, playing ukuleles or guitars and singing. One of the songs they played began:

"Oh, we're going to a hukilau
A huki, huki, hukilau. . . ."

The tune is very catchy, and Trippie found herself singing it over and over again. When Saturday arrived, the whole family was glad that the time had come actually to go to a hukilau with the Lahaina family.

In old Hawaii, the hukilau was a village event. The natives made a tremendous net of olona fibers. Some of the men would go out in their canoes and spread the huge net out in a circle. Long ropes, with ti leaves tied onto them like fly chasers, were attached to the net. The swishing leaves were supposed to attract the fish. When the net was full, everyone in the village helped to pull it in, and everyone shared in the big feast afterward.

The word hukilau comes from *huki* meaning pull, and *lau* meaning leaf.

The hukilau was great fun! Trippie and Jeff waded into the water to help pull in the net. There were not very many fish, but no one cared, because a luau had been prepared, including pig cooked in the imu, stewed

chicken, sweet potatoes, coconut pudding, fresh pineapple, and poi.

The modern hukilau is put on by the Samoan natives who belong to the nearby Mormon Temple. The money for the tickets goes to the church.

On the way home from the hukilau, the Allens stopped to visit the fabulous Mormon Temple, which was built in 1919 at a cost of $200,000. Not far away, they visited a quaint Japanese temple of the Buddhist faith. There are many different kinds of temples and churches in Hawaii, and many different religious beliefs.

Driving on, the Allens came to a head formed of natural stone on a cliff.

"Can you guess who this is?" asked Mr. Allen.

"It looks like George Washington, with the three-cornered hat," said Jeff.

"Right!" agreed his father. "And now it is called the George Washington Stone. But there is an old legend about this head that goes far back into history. They say a prince fell in love with a bird woman with magic powers. He promised to be faithful to her. But he failed, and she turned him into stone."

On their way back to the hotel, the Allens passed two important military points — Schofield Barracks, which is now a training center, and Hickam Field, a large air base. Then they came to the most important military point, Pearl Harbor, where World War II started.

"We'll take a boat trip to Pearl Harbor tomorrow," said Mr. Allen.

PEARL HARBOR — our Great Naval Station

Most visitors to the islands remember the terrible day on December 7, 1941, when Pearl Harbor was attacked by the Japanese.

Of course Trippie and Jeff were not born that long ago, but they knew all about World War II and how it began. They wanted very much to see our most important naval base in the Pacific.

On Monday afternoon the Allens boarded a sightseeing yacht with a group of other tourists and sailed out into the Pearl Harbor area. The captain of the yacht announced the points of interest, and gave them much information.

Trippie and Jeff learned that in about fifty years Pearl Harbor has grown from a small coaling station to a giant base, covering more than ten thousand acres of land and valued at over one and a half billion dollars. The Commander-in-Chief of the Pacific Fleet has headquarters in the Pearl Harbor area.

The naval shipyard's main job is to maintain and improve ships and submarines of the Navy. The shipyard has four dry docks, and more floating dry docks, where ships can be repaired. Besides, there are twenty-five shops for ship repair, alteration, and building.

The Allens saw many great navy ships tied to the

Pearl Harbor Naval Shipyard

OFFICIAL U. S. NAVY Photograph

docks, and some in the dry docks being repaired. They saw many large Navy buildings lining the shore, and giant cranes strong enough to lift a whole ship.

Soon they saw the Stars and Stripes flying in the breeze from a mast rising out of the water near the shore. The captain told them that, on the day of the Pearl Harbor attack, eighteen ships were sunk or damaged. Two great battleships, the *Arizona* and the *Utah*, went down with their crews.

The American flag flies from the mast of the *Arizona*, whose hull lies under water, where she was sunk. The men who went down with her are still there, because several attempts proved it impossible to bring them to the surface. What a grim reminder of World War II!

It took almost four years of fighting in the Pacific for the United States to defeat the Japanese. The young citizens of Hawaii of every race joined the war effort.

At first, young men of Japanese descent were looked upon with suspicion. But their loyalty was soon proved, and they joined the services in great numbers. They made a wonderful record all over the world.

LEI MAKERS' MARKET

"Tomorrow, we fly to the big island, Hawaii," said Mr. Allen. "We'll see some wonderful sights."

Early the next morning, the Allens packed some bags and drove to the airport.

As they got close to the airport, Trippie pointed. "Look at all those grass shacks with leis hanging on the walls," she said.

"This is the lei makers' market," said Mr. Allen. "Most of the beautiful leis that are sold at the airport are made here."

"Let's stop and get some leis," suggested Mrs. Allen.

Trippie and Jeff enjoyed watching a Hawaiian woman making her leis. She pierced each blossom with a long, sharp needle and slipped the flowers onto a string, one by one, much as you would string beads. She worked very quickly, because the leis must be sold while the flowers are fresh and crisp.

"When do you sell the most leis?" Trippie inquired.

The lei maker told her that she looks forward to the many festivals that are held on the islands. The most important is Lei Day, on the first of May, when great flower pageants are staged by all the schools. A beautiful outdoor pageant, with a king and queen, is held in downtown Honolulu. On that day, everyone wears at least one lei.

Another important day is June 11, Kamehameha I's birthday, when his statue in the Civic Center is draped with hundreds of beautiful leis. Aloha Week, in October, calls for thousands of leis too. But, of course, any day is a good day for wearing a lei in Hawaii. And with visitors arriving from all parts of the world daily, the lei makers dispose of their wares very quickly. Many leis are shipped to the mainland by air express.

HONOLULU
INTERNATIONAL AIRPORT

Arriving at the airport, Mr. Allen returned his car to the rental office there. "I can rent another car on the big island," he said.

"What an exciting place!" exclaimed Trippie, as the family entered the terminal. "I can see why they call it Honolulu *International* Airport."

A group of passengers had just arrived from the Orient. There were Hindu women wearing saris, and men wearing turbans; Chinese women with slim slit skirts; and many other Oriental people.

"My teacher told me that people call Hawaii the Crossroads of the Pacific," remarked Jeff. "Now I know what she meant."

"This is one of the busiest airports in the whole world," said his father. "I think that nearly a million people use this airport in a year."

Soon an announcement came over the loud-speaker: "Flight for island of Hawaii now loading at Gate 9."

The Allens stopped at Gate 9 to wave good-by to the hundreds of people who were standing to watch the planes take off and land.

"Aloha! Aloha!" came the calls of the friendly people.

The plane flew low over the sparkling blue sea, and

it seemed that just a few minutes had passed when the stewardess announced:

"To your left you can see the island of Molokai, the fifth in size of the Hawaiian Islands."

The Allens could see the island clearly. They could see high mountains and steep cliffs, with a quiet green valley below.

The voice went on: "Molokai is famous for the wonderful work of the Catholic priest, Father Damien, who gave his life for the leper colony. Today, with modern healing methods, many of the lepers have been cured. There are only about fifty people with active cases of leprosy left in the colony. Most of Molokai is used for raising pineapple or the taro plant from which poi is made. Cattle are raised here too."

Next the stewardess pointed out the small island of Lanai, which is all one vast pineapple plantation. Almost all of the twenty-five hundred people on the island work for the pineapple company, which has built them a modern city with comfortable houses, churches, movies, a hospital, and a recreation center. The State of Hawaii provides modern schools.

In just forty-five minutes the plane landed at the island of Maui. Some of the people got off the plane, but the Allens stayed on, as they were going on to the big island of Hawaii.

After the plane took off again, it flew over Maui,

the second island in size. The stewardess announced:

"Maui was named after the famous Hawaiian half-god, Maui. There are many legends about his daring deeds. One of the stories tells that he stood on the top of Haleakala, the great crater known as the House of the Sun. Here, he reached up and stopped the sun in its travels. He made it go more slowly, so that his mother could have more daylight to finish her tapa making."

Soon a tremendous mountain came into view.

"We are now flying over Haleakala, the House of the Sun," said the stewardess. "The whole top of the mountain is part of Hawaii National Park. Haleakala is the world's largest inactive volcano. The crater is seven miles long and more than twenty miles around. People drive, ride horseback, or hike up to the rim of Haleakala to watch the sunrise. It is one of the most beautiful sights in the world.

"Some people find time to take a horseback trip down into Haleakala Crater, and there are many interesting things to see.

"Within this immense crater, there are high crater cones taller than a New York skyscraper. There are caves, meadows, trees, and a rare plant found nowhere else. It is the silversword, a cactus with leaves that shine like silver. The center stalk towers as high as six to ten feet in full growth. Just once in its life, the tall stalk bursts into purple and yellow flowers. As soon as the flowers die, the plant begins to die too. It never blooms again."

The stewardess added: "In August 1958, a station for tracking satellites was opened near the western crest of Haleakala crater."

Soon the Allens heard: "To the far right is the island of Kahoolawe, the smallest of the Hawaiian group. No one lives there. It is used as a target island by United States ships and planes."

Haleakala Crater on island of Maui

HAWAII — the Big Island

Before long, the plane was flying over the island of Hawaii. The Allens could see a great spectacle below. Tremendous frothy white waterfalls were gushing over steep rock cliffs dropping sharply to the sea. Then, a short distance away, the extinct volcano, Mauna Kea, could be seen rising to fourteen thousand feet. It was capped with gleaming white snow.

"Mauna Kea," said the stewardess, "is one of the two great volcanic peaks which form the center of the big island. You shall see the other, Mauna Loa, the largest active volcano in the world, on your trip around the island."

Then, before the Allens realized it, the plane glided over the smooth harbor at Hilo, the principal city of the island of Hawaii, and landed at the modern airport.

Hilo is the second largest city in the islands, but small compared to Honolulu. Its population is only about twenty-five thousand.

Trippie and Jeff liked the looks of Hilo. It had modern stores, hotels, houses, schools, and a beautiful new public library. A great tidal wave struck Hilo in 1946, causing heavy damage, so much of the town had to be rebuilt.

"Hilo is known as the orchid capital of the world,"

said Mr. Allen. "I'll take you to one of the great orchid nurseries first."

What a sight the Allens saw! Dozens of different kinds of orchids growing in great masses, not in hothouses but right outdoors. They watched the orchids being picked, sorted, and made into leis and corsages. They learned that orchids are a multimillion-dollar industry in the islands. Orchids are shipped by air express all over the world.

An orchid nursery

From the orchid nursery, it was a short ride to famous Rainbow Falls. And what luck! The Allens arrived just in time to see a lovely rainbow shining through the rushing, misty falls.

From there, they started out for Kilauea Crater, the active volcano. They passed miles and miles of sugar fields. Then they started driving through mountain roads. Immense ferns, taller than a full-grown man, with stems as large as tree trunks, grew in thick clumps along the road.

"We are now in Hawaii National Park," said Mr. Allen.

"How can that be?" asked Jeff, puzzled. "The stewardess on the plane said Hawaii National Park was on the island of Maui."

"She was right," said Mr. Allen. "Haleakala Crater on Maui is included in the national park, but the largest part of the park is on the island of Hawaii."

The Allens paid a visit to the government bird park. Here they saw many of the rare island birds, including the tiny birds whose feathers were used in ancient feather cloaks. There were also many of the chattering black myna birds which are quite common in the islands, and the rare *nene*, a gooselike bird, which has been named Hawaii's official bird.

After a while, the Allens saw ahead of them an old hotel built of lava rock.

"There's the Volcano House," said Mr. Allen. "It sits right on the rim of Kilauea Crater. We are going to spend the night there."

From the glassed-in porch of the old Volcano House, the Allens saw a sight they would never forget! There before them was the huge spreading black crater. And it was in action! Great bursts of steam were rising from giant cracks in the earth, as far as the eyes could see.

Mrs. Allen looked worried. "Is it safe to stay here all night?" she asked.

"Of course," her husband assured her. "The steam doesn't mean that the volcano is erupting. The Hawaiian Volcano Observatory is always on watch and gives warnings in time if there is any danger of an eruption."

After a good night's rest, the Allens arose early and went to see the Thurston Lava Tube. Mr. Allen took a flashlight along, so they could see inside the long, dark tunnel, which was formed by several lava flows hardening over each other.

"It feels spooky," whispered Trippie, as they made their way over a narrow board walk and on through the tunnel.

"Let's stay close to each other," warned Mrs. Allen. "It would be easy to get lost in here."

When they came out of the tunnel, the Allens returned to the hotel and set out for the rest of their trip around the island.

"Now we will head for the Kona coast," said Mr. Allen. "There is a road along the ocean which will take us to the west side of the island."

Driving toward Kona, Trippie and Jeff were amazed to see the immense piles of black and brown lava rock. They were the remains of old lava flows, and they covered the whole side of Mauna Loa, from the crater to the ocean, about thirty miles away.

In the past hundred years, Mauna Loa has erupted twenty-nine times. Each time, great rivers of molten fire have steamed down the mountainside, destroying everything in the way—trees, plants, buildings. The fiery lava

Mauna Loa in action

was so hot that when it hit the sea, it set the water boiling.

At various places along the road, the Allens noticed markers topped with Hawaiian warrior heads. Each marker gave the date of that particular lava flow.

Trippie and Jeff got out of the car and picked up pieces of the lava rock for souvenirs.

Soon they came to a village that looked brand new. It was. Mauna Loa's eruption had swept away a whole village, and it had to be rebuilt.

As they drove along, Trippie and Jeff were amazed to see a beach that looked different from any they had ever seen before! It looked as though it were covered with shiny black coal dust. Mr. Allen stopped the car.

"This is the famous black sand beach in the Puma area," he explained. "The lava flow from the volcano turned the sand completely black."

Jeff took a handful of the black sand, wrapped it in a piece of paper, and said, "I'll take this back home, or else no one will believe I saw a beach of solid black sand."

The Kona coast is famous for its coffee. As the Allens continued on their trip, they could see the coffee trees loaded with red berries, growing along the sides of the hills.

"This coffee is about ready to be picked," said Mr. Allen. He stopped the car and picked a berry. He opened is up and showed Trippie and Jeff the inside. There were two coffee beans facing each other, inside a thin skin.

"These ripe coffee beans are soaked in water to soften and clean them," Mr. Allen explained. "Then women workers spread them on the ground with large rakes, to dry in the sun."

"After the coffee beans are dry," Mr. Allen went on, "they go to the mill, where the skin is taken off, and the beans are roasted and ground into coffee as we know it. Kona coffee is shipped all over the world."

KAILUA—Town of Legend

After a while, the Allens reached Kailua, the principal town of the Kona coast, nestled near a bay of fascinating beauty.

"Kamehameha I chose this beautiful spot to spend his old age," said Mr. Allen. "He was born not too far away, just north of the Kona area."

The Allens spent the night in a modern inn on the Kona shore. The next day they saw many interesting sights.

First, they took a boat ride to Kealakekua Bay. The captain of the boat pointed out a slim, tall monument erected to Captain Cook, the discoverer of the islands.

"Imagine!" exclaimed Jeff. "We are on the exact spot where Captain Cook was killed!"

Looking out on the deep blue water, Trippie asked: "What kind of boats are those out there?"

"Fishing boats," said the captain. "Sportsmen come here from all over the world to fish for giant marlin. One that was caught weighed more than a ton. Another had a whole one-hundred-and-fifty-pound tuna in his stomach."

"How about hunting?" asked Mr. Allen. "Are there any wild animals on the island?"

"Oh yes," said the captain. "On the upper slopes of the mountains, we can hunt wild goats, wild pigs, or wild sheep. We also hunt pheasant, quail, doves, and pigeons."

After the boat trip, the Allens set out in their car for more sight-seeing.

First, they stopped at a historic spot called the City of Refuge.

"It doesn't look like much to me," said Jeff. "All I see is a few big rocks."

"These few rocks are all that is left of a strong, thick wall that surrounded the ancient refuge," explained his father. "If a man was pursued by an enemy, he could find protection there. It was believed that once a man had reached the City of Refuge, he would be safe from his enemies even after he left the refuge."

The Allens saw, not far away, one of the old *heiaus*, or ancient temples, where religious rites were performed by the old Hawaiian priests called *kahunas*. While nothing remains of many of these heiaus except a few stones, this one had been rebuilt. There were a grass house and a tall tower built of tree trunks and branches, called the oracle tower.

"The whole life of the early natives revolved around these temples," said Mr. Allen. "There were ceremonies for birth, coming into manhood, marriage, and death. There were prayers held for the sick, prayers to the god of war for protection from enemies, prayers for crops, and many other occasions."

HAWAIIAN COWBOYS

"What a surprise I have for you now!" said Mr. Allen, as he began to drive inland.

After a while, Jeff suddenly blurted out: "Oh boy! I see cowboys!"

"Cowboys? You're dreaming!" retorted Trippie.

"Jeff is right," said Mr. Allen. "We're coming to a tremendous cattle ranch. It's second in size only to the famous King Ranch in Texas."

"Hawaii is the last place I imagine would have a cattle ranch," said Mrs. Allen.

"That's what most people think," her husband replied, "but actually, there are more than two hundred ranches on the big island, covering nearly a million acres. They produce over a hundred thousand head of beef cattle."

Jeff wanted to know how cattle ranching started in the islands.

"Captain Vancouver brought the first cattle during the reign of Kamehameha I," said his father. "The king's order—that none of the cattle were to be killed for ten years—increased the numbers greatly. Some of these cattle escaped and roamed wild for some years. When a sailor named John Palmer Parker left his ship in 1815 and decided to settle in Hawaii, the king asked him to hunt some of the cattle which were roaming wild. Parker built up herds from the wild cattle, and this was the beginning of the great ranch."

"Where did they get the cowboys?" asked Jeff.

"At first, Parker brought cowboys from Mexico. But the Hawaiians loved horses, and soon more and more Hawaiians became *paniolas*, which is the name for cowboys in the islands."

"Do they ride and rope and play guitars like our Western cowboys do?" asked Jeff.

"Yes," said his father, "and at branding time they have real Western-style roundups. I hear they add a touch of their own though. They wear flower leis on their hats."

BACK TO HONOLULU

That evening, the Allens flew back to Honolulu.

"It's too bad we won't have time to visit the island of Kauai," said Mr. Allen. "If we were going there, we would have to change to another plane out of Honolulu, going north."

Mr. Allen showed Jeff and Trippie the island of Kauai on the airline map. "Kauai is so beautiful that people call it the garden isle," he said. Pointing to the map again, Mr. Allen added, "This tiny island west of Kauai is Niihau. The island is privately owned, and nobody can visit there unless he is specially invited."

The Allens spent the next two days in Honolulu, dividing their time between the beach and in shopping for gifts and souvenirs of the arts and crafts of the islands. Trippie bought herself a hula skirt and Jeff bought a ukulele. Together, they bought records of island music.

"Now we can put on our own hula show," said Trippie.

Most people who come to Hawaii by ship, return to the mainland by plane, and that is just what the Allens did.

As their plane took off, they all looked back at the airport, and the last word they saw was ALOHA on the

airport tower. The word had an even more loving and tender meaning for them now.

Looking down at the ocean under them, they could see leis floating on the water.

"One of the big ships has just left the harbor," said Mr. Allen. "When people leave by ship, it is a custom to throw their leis overboard. If the lei floats to shore, it's a sign that the person will return to Hawaii."

"I know I'm going to return someday," said Trippie confidently.

"I'm coming back for sure," said Jeff.

PAU   (The End)

HAWAIIAN WORDS in This Book

There are only twelve letters in the Hawaiian alphabet — the five vowels and seven consonants: *h k l m n p w*. Occasionally the letter *t* is used in addition. All the consonants have the same sound as in English, with the exception of *w* which is sometimes sounded like *v*, but usually like our English *w*. The vowels have the Latin sounds:

a as *ah*, as in *harm*	Each vowel is usually sounded separately,
e as *ay*, as in *they*	except for these combinations:
i as *ee*, as in *machine*	*ae* or *ai*, as in *eye*
o as *oh*, as in *hold*	*au* as *ow*, as in *cow*
u as *oo*, as in *moon*	*ei* as *ay*, as in *weigh*

The accent usually falls on the next to the last syllable.

Word	Pronunciation	Meaning
Akoni	ah-*koh*-nee	Hawaiian name for Anthony
ali'i	ah-lee-ee	ruling class in early Hawaii
aloha	ah-*loh*-hah	hello or good-by
aloha oe	ah-*loh*-hah *oh*-ay	greeting with affection
hala	*hah*-lah	the tree from which woven mats, bags, and hats are made
Haleakala	hah-lay-ah-*kah*-lah	extinct volcanic crater
haole	hah-*oh*-lay	man or woman of white race
Hawaii	hah-*wy*-ee	name of largest island
Hawaiian	hah-*wy*-yan	pertaining to Hawaii
Hawaii Loa	hah-*wy*-ee *loh*-ah	early discoverer of the islands
heiau	hay-ee-ow	ancient temple
Hilo	*hee*-loh	city on island of Hawaii
holomu	*hoh*-loh-moo	fitted long dress
Honolulu	hoh-noh-*loo*-loo	capital of the islands
hukilau	*hoo*-kee-low	village fishing party
hula	*hoo*-lah	Hawaiian dance
humu-humu-nuku-nuku-apu-aa	*hoo*moo-*hoo*moo-*noo*koo-*noo*koo-ah-*poo*-*ah*-ah	a tiny Hawaiian fish

124

imu	*ee*-moo	underground oven
Iolani	ee-oh-*lah*-nee	palace in Honolulu
kahili	kah-*hee*-lee	a decorated pole
Kahoolawe	kah-hoo-*lah*-way	small target island
kahuna	kah-*hoo*-nah	ancient priest
Kailua	ky-*loo*-ah	town in Kona
Kala	kah-lah	name for Carl
Kalakaua	kah-lah-*kow*-ah	the "merry" monarch
kamaaina	kah-mah-*y*-nah	old resident of Hawaii
Kamehameha	kah-*may*-hah-*may*-hah	name of five kings
Kauai	kow-*wy*	most northern island
Kawaiahao	kah-*wy*-ah-*hah*-oh	old church in Honolulu
Kealakekua	kay-*ah*-lah-kay-*koo*-ah	bay on Kona coast
keikis	*kay*-kees	children
Kilani	kee-*lah*-nee	woman's name
Kilauea	kee-lah-oo-*ay*-ah	volcano on island of Hawaii
Kiwalao	kee-wah-*lah*-oh	early Hawaiian king
koa	*koh*-ah	a Hawaiian tree
Kona	koh-nah	west coast of Hawaii
kukui	koo-*koo*-ee	a nut used for oil
Lahaina	lah-*hy*-nah	a family name
Lanai	lah-*nah*-ee	the pineapple island; also a porch
lauhala	low-*hah*-la	woven matting
lau lau	low-low	meat or fish in ti-leaf jacket
lava lava	*lah*-vah *lah*-vah	a wrap-around skirt
lei	lay	wreath of flowers
Liholiho	*lee*-hoh-*lee*-hoh	prince who became *Kamehameha II*
Liliuokalani	*lee*-lee-oo-o-kah-*lah*-nee	last queen of Hawaii
Loika	loh-*ee*-kah	name for Lois
luau	*loo*-ow	an island feast
Luka	*loo*-kah	name for Luke
Lunalilo	loo-nah-*lee*-loh	prince elected to rule islands
mahi mahi	*mah*-hee-*mah*-hee	dolphin
malihini	mah-lee-*hee*-nee	newcomer to the islands
malo	mah-loh	a loin cloth
Maui	*mow*-ee	second largest island
Mauna Kea	*mow*-nah kay-ah	mountain on Hawaii
Mauna Loa	*mow*-nah *loh*-ah	active volcano on Hawaii
mele	*may*-lay	a religious chant

Menehune	may-nay-*hoo*-nay	dwarf people
Molokai	*moh*-loh-*kah*-ee	fifth island in size
muu muu	*moo-moo*	a long, loose dress
nene	*nay-nay*	official Hawaiian bird
Niihau	*nee-ee*-how	a privately owned island
Nuuanu Pali	noo-oo-*ah*-noo-*pah*-lee	cliff above Nuuanu valley
Oahu	oh-*ah*-hoo	third largest island
olona	oh-*loh*-nah	a plant with strong fibers
opu	*oh*-poo	stomach or abdomen
paniola	pah-nee-*oh*-lah	Hawaiian cowboy
pa'u	pah-oo	early Hawaiian skirt
pau	pow	the end; finished
Pele	*pay*-lay	goddess of fire
pikake	pee-*kah*-kee	flower we know as jasmine
pili	*pee*-lee	grass used for early houses
poi	poy	paste made from taro plant
tapa	*tah*-pah	cloth pounded from bark; sometimes called *kapa*
taro	*tah*-roh	a root vegetable
ukulele	oo-koo-*lay*-lay	a stringed instrument
Waikiki	wy-kee-*kee*	famous beach at Oahu
wiliwili	*wee*-lee-*wee*-lee	a supple wood

Island children in Aloha Week Court scene

HAWAIIAN FLAG. Designed for King Kamehameha the Great, in 1812. This has been the flag of the kingdom, the brief republic, and the territory. Now it is the flag of the State of Hawaii. The eight white, red, and blue stripes stand for the eight main Hawaiian islands. The English Jack in the corner is a tribute to British explorers who discovered the islands.

ROYAL COAT OF ARMS

This is the ancient royal Coat-of-Arms, from which the Seal of Hawaii was adapted.

SEAL OF HAWAII

Adopted by the Territory of Hawaii in 1901. Now the word "Territory" is changed to "State".